MW01299503

WRITE YOUR FEARS AWAY

* * *

How writing your worst-case
scenarios can reduce your anxiety

David Barnhart, EdD CCMHC

Publisher's Note

This publication is designed to provide helpful information on the subject matter presented. This workbook is not sold for the purpose of providing psychological, mental health or other services. If counseling or psychological services are needed, the services of a licensed professional provider should be sought.

Copyright © 2010 David L. Barnhart
Dr. Barnhart's Cycling Photo by Melanie Backer

All rights reserved.

No part of this publication may be reproduced, stored in a retrieval system, or transmitted in any form or by any means electronic, mechanical, photocopying, recording, or otherwise without the prior permission of the author.

ISBN: 1449977189
ISBN-13: 9781449977184

Dedication

To all my clients over the years who have had the courage to collaborate with me in counseling as they faced their fears and risked uncertain outcomes to attain inner peace and good relationships with family, friends, and coworkers.

Contents

Acknowledgements vii
Introduction ix

PART 1
ANXIETY, TRIGGERS, AND REACTIONS 1

Chapter 1 3
    Anxiety and Anxiety Disorders 3
    The feeling of anxiety 5
    Exercise: Fifteen minutes of worry writing 6

Chapter 2 9
    Triggers, Avoidance, and Worry 9

Chapter 3 11
    Natural Avoidance and Habituation 11
    Exercise: What do you do to avoid anxiety? 12

Chapter 4 13
    Worry as a Compulsion 13
    Exercise: How much do you worry? 14
    Example: 14

PART 2
FACING YOUR FEARS THROUGH EXPOSURE 15

Chapter 5 17
Effective Treatment 17
Facing your fears through exposure 17
Exercise: What fears have you overcome? 18
Intrusive thoughts, urges, and anxiety triggers 18
Exercise: Identify intrusive thoughts 20
Exercise: Keep a stress log 21

PART 3
YOUR WRITTEN EXPOSURE 23

Chapter 6 25
Preparing to Write Your Fears 25
Client writing examples 26
Examples of writing triggers and worst-case scenarios 26
Exercise: Identify your anxiety triggers 31
Writing Instructions 33
Exercise: Write your fears 34

PART 4
KEEPING YOUR FEARS AT BAY 35

Chapter 7 37
Relapse Prevention 37
Identifying and Changing Dysfunctional Thinking with GOFAR 38
Exercise: Develop your relapse prevention plan 44

Closing 45
Appendix 47
Writing your fears note pages 47

Acknowledgements

In August 2008, I had the privilege of attending the Behavior Therapy Institute in Palo Alto, California, which was conducted by the International OCD Foundation[1]. A number of experts in the treatment of obsessive compulsive disorder (OCD) and obsessive compulsive spectrum disorders presented the latest information on treatment. The attendees received encouragement to follow validated treatment models. Most helpful, was the opportunity afforded us to engage in consultation with the experts. Dr. Eda Gorbis[2] led the breakout group I attended.

Eda Gorbis, PhD, MFCC, who has a private practice and is an assistant clinical professor at the UCLA School of Medicine, taught her group how to write out their fears. She told us to take our pens and write out all of our worst fears and worries for the next fifteen minutes. Skeptical about what this would do, I surprised myself when I wrote for fifteen minutes and did not repeat the same worries. I realized after a few days that when I thought about my worst fears, they didn't seem to evoke much discomfort. Over the course of the last year, I have asked many of my clients to write out their worst fears. Virtually all have benefitted from this exercise. Those with anxiety disorders who followed the prescription and wrote diligently experienced a dramatic drop in their overall anxiety. However, my other clients, those without a clinical level of anxiety also benefitted. Their experience was similar to my own. Even a relatively small amount of time spent writing out fears makes a significant difference in reducing the amount of time spent in rumination about stressful circumstances. Several clients have told me they have adopted the practice of writing out their worst-case scenario fears as soon as a new concern develops. Many have found that facing the worst-case scenario early suppresses the negative emotions that may have commonly developed into worried rumination in the past.

Dr. Gorbis went well beyond the standard number of consultations for participants in the Behavior Therapy Institute. She took my calls on a regular weekly basis until I had a complete grasp of the importance of exposure in reducing anxiety. I asked Dr. Gorbis where I could read more about her writing technique.[3] She told me, "I'm telling you now how to do it." I thought it would be helpful to create a guide for my clients and patients. I have used various iterations of this guide, and our clients and patients have found it a helpful reference as they complete their homework. If you find it helpful, thank Dr. Gorbis for her work.

My colleagues, Dave Stephens, Jessica Cleveland, and Lee Ann Penman have used various iterations of this workbook with their clients. Dr. Judy Park, Marvin Kalachman, and Dr. Tom Tenbrunsel have consulted over lunch many times as we talked about the use of written exposure with our clients and have entrusted us with referrals of clients and patients suffering with anxiety and anxiety disorders. Dr. Aparna Vuppala, my colleague and a child and adolescent psychiatrist, has been attentive to the children and adolescents with anxiety disorders to encourage their families to follow through with cognitive behavior therapy and by providing the psychiatric care they need. I love working with you all and collaborating with you on our client and patient care. Thank you to all of the administrative staff that make it possible for all of us to focus on our work, Arlene and Bill Butler, Joanne Hilst, Christi White, and Dennis Cornelison.

Thank you, Donna Barnhart, for your support during the last forty-two years of marriage. You've run our offices, our home, reared a PhD son and an MD daughter (David and Melanie), watched over my father's terminal care, and cared for my mother during a very difficult time. You are clearly the best person I've ever known. You bless my life everyday with your presence.

David L. Barnhart, EdD, CCMHC, NCC

Introduction

Your interest in this workbook may come from a desire to reduce everyday stress and anxiety, simple curiosity about the subject, or maybe you have a friend or family member whose anxiety seems to be turned up a little higher than that of most people you know. The techniques included are used as tools by clinical counselors to help clients with anxiety disorders reduce anxiety to achieve long-lasting effects. I'm excited to present this information to you because even my clients without anxiety disorders helped me see the long-term benefits that can be achieved in the everyday stress people experience at work, at home, and in relationships.

You don't need to have an anxiety disorder to benefit from this work. If you do suffer from an anxiety disorder, I recommend that you consult with a clinical counselor, social worker, marriage and family therapist, or psychologist in addition to using this workbook. I believe the support, expertise, and accountability provided by an experienced therapist will tend to save you time, money, and discomfort in the long run.

PART 1

* * *

ANXIETY, TRIGGERS, AND REACTIONS

Chapter 1

Anxiety and Anxiety Disorders

If you haven't lived with an anxiety disorder, you can still be sympathetic. As a human being you've experienced some level of anxiety from time to time. It may have been mild like when you forgot to study for that midterm exam. Perhaps you felt butterflies in the pit of your stomach, you had difficulty falling asleep because of worry, your palms became sweaty, or your heart rate increased. You may have experienced quite a surge of adrenaline when suddenly out of the dark of night in your rear view mirror you see a police cruiser with its blue lights flashing. If you felt that same hot flush with heart pounding, dry mouth, and sweaty palms from out of nowhere for no apparent reason, you know how a panic attack feels. In panic disorder that feeling comes unexpectedly at any time and is repeated at random intervals. The shock and discomfort of high anxiety will cause a person to avoid situations where they fear having a panic attack. In extreme cases people with panic disorder don't dare venture outside their homes.

Working with people suffering from anxiety or an anxiety disorder provides some of the most gratifying experiences for clinicians. By teaching some useful tools, counselors get to see a real, long-lasting transformation with successful treatment. Moderate to severe anxiety can cause people extreme difficulty in completing everyday tasks. Concentration, decision making, coping with every day stress, and the ability to relax or fall asleep may become impaired. This can begin a downward spiral of physical and mental fatigue leading to a loss of interest in daily activities and even depression. Fortunately, people with anxiety disorders treated with cognitive behavior therapy can significantly reduce anxiety, a change in the brain that continues after therapy ends.[4][5] Medications such as selective serotonin reuptake inhibitors (SSRIs) can also ameliorate some of the uncomfortable physical symptoms of anxiety enabling anxiety sufferers to function better as long as they continue taking medication. Most people prefer not to take medication or to take as little medication as necessary. If there is a way to learn to cope with or reduce anxiety through their own effort, that is their preference.

Anxiety can be evoked by many factors, none of which are elective. People don't choose to have anxiety. Sometimes extreme events such as war, sexual and physical abuse, traumatic loss of a loved one or associate, natural disasters, or even drug use and medications may precipitate anxiety or an anxiety disorder. Names for some of these anxiety disorders include post traumatic stress disorder (PTSD), panic disorder, and acute stress disorder. Sometimes, people may be genetically predisposed to anxiety. However, people can develop anxiety disorders such as obsessive-compulsive disorder, social phobia (social anxiety), specific phobia, separation anxiety, or generalized anxiety disorder without any obvious family history. Intrusive thoughts, flashbacks (memories of traumatic events), guilt feelings and even shame make people with these disorders hide their inner turmoil from others, and they often fail to get needed help. If their disorder interferes significantly with their ability to function, they may come to the attention of their physician or seek a consult with a counselor.

Being given a diagnosis often brings great relief for people with anxiety disorders. For some, they are relieved to learn they are not "crazy." For most, they just wanted to know there is a treatment, and they can get better. They often want to know "what are my chances for getting better?" With OCD, which is one of the most difficult to treat disorders, studies indicate a 75 percent probability of significant improvement through cognitive behavior therapy. Research also shows that only 20 percent of individuals who receive cognitive therapy suffer from acute and post-traumatic stress symptoms after six months, as compared to 67 percent who only receive supportive counseling.[6] Other studies looking at PTSD and generalized anxiety disorder (GAD) indicate that when exposure therapy (purposely subjecting oneself to an anxiety-provoking situation), is included as a part of cognitive behavior therapy for approximately sixteen to twenty sessions a 50 percent reduction of symptoms may be achieved.[7] The efficacy of cognitive behavioral therapy is also well documented for treatment of panic disorder. Research reveals that by week six of treatment, approximately 76 percent of compliant individuals see a reduction in panic symptoms and by eleven weeks may be ready to reduce or end therapy.[8] Medication and relaxation procedures used to treat panic disorder, when compared to cognitive behavioral therapy over a three-month period, have not been found to be as successful for panic disorder. However, recent studies reveal that after only three months of cognitive therapy (the equivalent of eleven to twelve weeks), a significant reduction of panic symptoms is evident.[9] With social and other specific phobias even Internet-delivered cognitive behavior therapy has shown a 65 percent approximate improvement rate, and that is with minimal therapist contact.[10] Individuals with separation anxiety have also reported improvement with the use of both familiy-based and individually based cognitive approaches.[11]

These changes appear to make long-lasting differences in the brain function of anxiety sufferers. For those who may be encouraged to do the challenging work of bearing the anxiety of exposure and response prevention and the work of cognitive restructuring, there is ample evidence of changes occurring in the brain as the result of cognitive behavior therapy.[12] Brain studies involving cerebral blood flow and the medial prefrontal cortex during anticipatory anxiety have shown that reductions in blood flow while performing a variety of cognitive tasks (i.e., writing) is evident. A reduction in blood flow is an indicator of lower levels of anxiety. The research shows that practice of tasks such as anticipating a shock to the fingers actually decreases blood flow in the brain and lowers anxiety levels.[13] In studies of social phobia, panic disorder, and post traumatic stress, researchers have found that using emotional regulation techniques like those taught in cognitive behavioral therapy produce greater cognitive-control responses (i.e., right dorsolateral prefrontal cortex) in patients.[14] For those suffering from PTSD, researchers have found a reciprocal relationship between blood flow in the medial prefrontal cortex and amygdala function in neutral and traumatic activity. Symptom severity was noted to decrease in the medial frontal cortex for both male veterans and female nurse veterans diagnosed with PTSD.[15]

So, the good news is that people can manage, reduce, or eliminate the interference of anxiety in their lives just like others manage, reduce, or eliminate the interference of diabetes, coronary artery disease, or some other physical ailment. We can benefit from counseling, coaching, education, and behavior change in dealing with mental health just as people have learned to manage their physical health.

The feeling of anxiety

The most important function our brains perform in addition to keeping lungs breathing and hearts beating is to protect us. Anxiety (fight or flight) is a self-protective response to a physical or psychological threat. In this mind-body experience, our whole physical being goes on a state of alert. We usually discriminate between fear and anxiety even though the emotional and physiological experience may be the same. Fear occurs when there is an actual physical threat. Anxiety may be more anticipated than immediate. In high anxiety, heart rate increases, respiration rate goes up, palms can feel sweaty, and the mouth can go dry. Some people feel like they must be having a heart attack. The discomfort associated with anxiety can range from minimal symptoms to mild, moderate, or severe symptoms. Clinically, we ask our clients to describe their anxiety's intensity in subjective units of discomfort (SUD) ranging on a scale from one to ten. A rating of one is almost no discomfort, and a ten represents the equivalent feeling of facing a bear. Minimal levels of anxiety may be dismissed quite easily for people without anxiety disorders (SUDs of one to three), but for those with anxiety disorders, even minimal symptoms can escalate into intense feelings (SUDs of seven to ten). This may lead to a perpetual state of worry and exhaustion at times.

Exercise: Fifteen minutes of worry writing

One of the things we learn in counseling and psychotherapy is that we can't change what we don't monitor. Clients who benefit the most from cognitive behavior therapy take notes, do homework, and get into the habit of writing down on paper or computer their thoughts, feelings, triggers for anxiety, plans, and goals. They learn to be open and honest about their experiences and collaborate in treatment. Overcoming anxiety requires hard work. To help you get into the swing of writing and becoming aware of your anxiety, triggers, and reactions, I suggest you begin with the same exercise I did when I worked with Dr. Gorbis. Take fifteen minutes to write about all your worries and fears.

After you've written for fifteen minutes, read what you've written, and note any themes that run through your writing. What are the particular thoughts, people, feelings, or situations that trigger anxiety and worry for you?

Themes:

Triggers (thoughts, people, situations, or feelings)

Chapter 2

Triggers, Avoidance, and Worry

While there can be actual threats to our physical well-being, most of the threats we experience in daily life come from perceived potential loss of our status among our peers and family. This explains why concern over what other people may think can ramp up anxiety in folks who have anxiety disorders. Concern over what others may think can elicit mild (SUDs one to three), moderate (SUDs four to six), or severe anxiety (SUDs seven to ten) in people who suffer from OCD or social phobia.

People without anxiety disorders commonly have the same or similar anxiety triggers (intrusive thoughts and events) as those with anxiety disorders. However, because their anxiety baseline isn't as high, they can more easily move on without much difficulty. For those with a higher baseline of anxiety, stressful events can result in diffuse physiological arousal and even panic attacks. This makes a threat trigger almost impossible for them to set aside. In reaction to their intense discomfort, anxiety sufferers often engage in avoidance behavior. Instinctually, we avoid situations that we believe make us feel uncomfortable or threatened. Avoidance commonly takes the form of leaving or staying away from a situation, distracting oneself by trying to think about other things, staying busy, or engaging in worry. Avoidance brings immediate relief but doesn't solve the problem. Until we face the fearful situation, we will contend with anxiety. Exposure to the anxiety-provoking situation, the very thing we try to avoid, offers the only long-lasting relief short of being medicated indefinitely.

The socially phobic person will avoid specific social situations and often justifies his avoidance as a lack of interest in the activity. The obsessive compulsive person will engage in physical or mental compulsions to reduce their anxiety. Some will use alcohol or illicit drugs to get anxiety relief, as well. Substance use tends to make the disorder worse in the long run, despite providing immediate relief. *The paradox for the anxiety sufferer: avoidance maintains anxiety* by keeping its victim from habituating or getting used to the anxiety-provoking situation. People without anxiety disorders *habituate* or get used to perceived threats much more quickly because they don't experience the intense discomfort of those with anxiety disorders. Let's think about how habituation works in the normal course of development.

Chapter 3

Natural Avoidance and Habituation

As babies and toddlers, human beings naturally tend to reference or cling to their parents when they enter a strange environment or if approached by a stranger. You've probably witnessed this. A mother holding a baby about nine months of age is approached by an old friend (a stranger to the baby) who exclaims, "Oh, this is your baby. How cute!" As the stranger approaches, the baby turns its face into its mother's bosom. This is a natural self-protective response (avoidance). Over time, as the baby is exposed to more strangers, his face will brighten when he gets positive attention from new adults. The baby learns through experience that these strangers won't hurt him, and he gets used to strangers making a fuss over him. We call this *habituation*. For those children whose anxiety is tuned up to a higher level, the discomfort doesn't let up as easily. They don't have the experience of anxiety dissipating quickly when they remain in social situations. Therefore, they may resist going to school or spending the night away from home. They worry about bad things happening to their mothers and fathers or going home and finding their parents gone. They may seek reassurance repeatedly. Unfortunately, reassurance doesn't solve the problem any better than avoidance. The only relief they know comes from avoidance. Avoidance is self-reinforcing and simply begets more avoidance, which leaves little opportunity for habituation.

Avoidance takes on many forms. Common forms of avoidance include seeking reassurance, worry, substance use, distracting one's self, or mental rituals such as counting, praying, and balancing bad thoughts with good thoughts. Through repetition and the self-reinforcing result of short-term relief from anxiety, these behaviors can become compulsions. That is, the urge to engage in the avoidance behavior grows to be strong and automatic.

Exercise: What do you do to avoid anxiety?

Do you observe any avoidance activity in your own life? Are there situations, people, or events that you skirt in order to keep your stress or anxiety down? Do you use substances to relax before approaching events or situations? Do you notice any mental rituals or habits you use to keep anxiety in check? Write any avoidance behavior you notice in yourself in the space below.

Chapter 4

Worry as a Compulsion

Another common reaction to an anxiety trigger is worry. We don't usually think of worry as a compulsion. Worrying seems like something we'd try to avoid as opposed to an avoidance technique. When faced with a potential threat or trigger, our brains attempt to find a solution. Using our imaginations, we think about possible outcomes, including worst-case scenarios. Even though feelings associated with worry are uncomfortable, those feelings peek with the trigger and usually become less intense simply because our brains eventually signal the release of hormones that reduce the intensity of the fight-or-flight response (anxiety/fear). Sometimes, coping thoughts are mixed in with worry. Coping thoughts generate more positive feelings. So, the natural lessening of intensity plus coping thoughts become associated with anxiety reduction. Therefore, the mental behavior of worry becomes strengthened through a process known as *negative reinforcement*. Negative reinforcement occurs when we engage in a behavior that is associated with a decrease in discomfort. In this case the cognitive behavior of worry is associated with a decrease in anxiety, and the tendency to worry becomes strengthened. The behavior used to reduce anxiety can make absolutely no rational sense (like counting ceiling tiles), or it may seem quite logical (worrying about what we'd do if the worst happens). Unfortunately, these behaviors don't provide an actual solution to reducing anxiety in the long term. Worry is not problem solving.

The *Merriam-Webster Online Dictionary* provides a couple of definitions for the verb *worry*. Think about this "to touch or disturb something repeatedly; to change the position of or adjust by repeated pushing or hauling"[16] These definitions remind me of a behavior common in OCD in which the person compulsively shifts or moves objects to line them up or puts them "just so" in order to reduce their anxiety. Worry is that mental tendency to move a situation around, think about it *just so* in order to feel better.

It would is not reasonable to think that we should try to never worry or that those of us who practice a religious faith should stop praying. For people with anxiety disorders, physical and mental attempts to cope can become compulsive behaviors that keep them in a loop of triggers and compulsions that become dysfunctional.

Manifestations of anxiety disorders can wax and wane over time in different people. Stress and acute stress from trauma can be associated with such manifestations, but stress is not always clearly a precursor. For example, OCD symptoms often manifest in the teens and twenties but not always. We also see OCD symptoms showing up in four-year-olds and forty-year-olds. Sometimes the symptoms worsen with stress, and sometimes they don't. Without treatment, however, symptoms tend to persist. With treatment, most individuals will attain long-lasting and significant relief.

Exercise: How much do you worry?

Track your worry and anxiety triggers for a few days. See if there are specific topics that come up and write them below in the middle column. In the right-hand column just enter tally marks to keep track of the frequency.

Example:

Date	Worry Topic	Frequency Tally
8/28/10	Children's friends	†††† 1
	Finances	111
	Lack of intimacy in marriage	1
8/29/10	Children's friends	111
	Finances	1111
	Lack of intimacy in marriage	†††† †††† 1
	Car falling apart	111

Your worries:

Date	Worry Topic	Frequency Tally

PART 2

* * *

FACING YOUR FEARS THROUGH EXPOSURE

Chapter 5

Effective Treatment

Effective treatment for anxiety disorders often includes cognitive behavior therapy. Medications, usually psychotropics called selective serotonin reuptake inhibitors (SSRIs), can be used to reduce anxiety in OCD, as well as other anxiety disorders. About 60-65 percent of clients with OCD get some relief of symptoms with SSRIs. Obsessions become more easily pushed aside, and compulsions become easier to resist. If medication is the only treatment, clients will usually relapse after a couple of weeks when medication is discontinued. About 75 percent of clients with OCD will get some long-lasting benefit if they receive cognitive behavior therapy specifically when treated with exposure and response prevention (ERP). Many clients with just about any anxiety disorder, including panic disorder, PTSD, and phobias, often should be treated with CBT including exposure.

Facing your fears through exposure

In order to habituate to an anxiety-provoking situation or trigger, it is necessary to place yourself in the situation or expose yourself to the trigger frequently for increasingly longer periods of time until habituation occurs. Exposure must take place without engaging in any compulsive ritual or avoidance behavior. Even though we take small steps, this is hard work. Imagine facing that bear in the woods because you choose to. Not only that, but you have to stay with that bear for at least ninety minutes or until your fear subsides by at least 50 percent. Tomorrow, repeat the process and continue repeating that for the next fifteen days. Anxiety clients must be highly motivated to follow through. We ask clients to resist (called *response prevention*) any compulsions that they've used in the past to reduce to their anxiety. Fortunately, we can design an approach to exposure that allows clients to take small steps, or we can create conditions that make exposure more tolerable. Make no mistake—this is challenging work. It will not be easy to do.

Exposure may be accomplished by having the client face the actual feared situation in real life (in vivo exposure) or in a contrived or imagined situation (imaginal exposure). For a person with a fear of heights, in vivo exposure may include gradually climbing and staying at specified heights until his fear subsides (habituation). Or, his counselor may ask him to imagine standing and looking off a balcony or cliff repeatedly until he habituates. Today, with computers, video exposure can provide virtual reality as well. Many times, our clients find YouTube exposure quite helpful. That is, you can find just about anything you can imagine on www.youtube.com: medical procedures, crowds of people, individuals throwing up, use of a Neti pot, or turbulence in an airplane—just name it and search. Likewise, a person with a fear of contamination, as in some clients with OCD, may be asked to touch a wet toilet seat and not wash his hands (in vivo exposure) or imagine touching a wet toilet seat and not washing his hands (imaginal exposure).

Exercise: What fears have you overcome?

See how natural exposure has worked in your life. This may encourage you to take the matter of exposure and habituation into your own hands. Most of us can remember a time in our lives when we fretted, worried, or had anxiety about different circumstances. You may have had a fear that something was lurking in your closet or under your bed. Take a few minutes and write down any fears that you may have had but no longer harbor. See if you can identify what may have happened in your thinking or experience that helped you "get over" that fear or worry.

_____
_____
_____
_____
_____
_____
_____
_____
_____

Intrusive thoughts, urges, and anxiety triggers

In vivo exposure becomes challenging when the fear attaches to an intrusive thought such as "My children will become failures because I'm not a good mother. I don't play with them or hug them enough." Everybody has intrusive, irrational thoughts like "I should smack your face!" However, without an anxiety disorder, these thoughts don't elicit self-recriminating thinking or compulsive rituals. "I should smack your face!" isn't acted out and doesn't elicit a high level of anxiety. In people without anxiety disorders, they recognize the irrational thought and simply move on. Here are some examples of random, intrusive thoughts clients with anxiety disorders have shared with me and others:

"Damn!" An intrusive curse like this may be followed by a compulsive prayer or other mental ritual. Sometimes the prayer must be said over until the person feels better or must be repeated if it's not said exactly right. Content like this may follow. "Please, Lord, forgive me for saying that word. I must be a bad person to have that word just come into my head. I could go to hell. Please forgive me for saying…the opposite of heaven…I really don't know why I have those thoughts. I'm trying to do better. Please help me. Amen."

"What if I picked up that knife and stabbed my children. What is wrong with me that I have these terrible thoughts? I must be a horrible person. What if I sleep walk in the night and get a knife out of the drawer and hurt my children? I've got to hide these knives so that I can't find them if I sleep walk." Intrusive thoughts such as this may be followed by hiding the kitchen knives and locking doors to make it difficult to get to the knives.

A siren sounds (a trigger). "What if my husband has been in a wreck? It's about time for him to come home. I need to call and check on him and make sure he is okay. Oh! I got his voicemail. He may be hurt and can't answer the phone. I have to keep calling until I get him. I'll call his office and see if he has left yet." Repeated calling and checking (compulsions) may follow.

Departure of loved ones for work or school (triggers) may be preceded by compulsive questioning and the superstitious (magical thinking) behavior of telling the person to be careful (compulsion). Failure to remind loved ones to be careful could result in something bad happening to them.

Social anxiety may be triggered by what most would consider innocuous events, yet they evoke thoughts such as "She's looking at me. I wonder if she's mad at me. Did I say something to hurt her feelings? I think I haven't told her I love her today. She probably thinks I don't care. I need to ask her if she's upset with me. What if I die with her being upset with me?" These thoughts may elicit the behavior of repeatedly seeking reassurance or apologizing for any perceived nuance of unkindness.

Exercise: Identify intrusive thoughts

As noted above, we all have intrusive thoughts from time to time. Write some of your intrusive thoughts. Some may be humorous and others, anxiety provoking. Are there situations that trigger intrusive thinking, e.g., socializing, being alone, or playing with kids?

Intrusive Thoughts	Situations that Trigger Intrusive Thoughts

Exercise: Keep a stress log

Those of us in the behavior-change business know that behavior change is hard. However, just as physical exercise produces strength and endurance, cognitive-behavioral exercise produces strength and endurance. As you now know, you can't change thinking, emotions, or behavior that you don't monitor. Therefore, the first step is to begin monitoring your cognitive behavior.

In this exercise, notice when your stress increases, when you have an anxiety-provoking urge, or anxiety trigger. For the next week, carry a pocket-size notebook or write in your PDA the following information (we call this a stress log):

Trigger	Emotional Feeling	Thoughts	SUD Level

1. When you notice an increase in your feelings of stress or anxiety, estimate your stress level and enter a number on a scale from one to ten in the SUD LEVEL column, where one represents very little stress and ten represents as much stress as you could possibly stand.
2. When you notice an increase in your stress or anxiety, write a brief description of the stress TRIGGER. You may experience a sudden increase in tension or anxiety but may not readily identify the trigger. In that case, describe what was happening at the time.
3. Now, describe your emotional feeling and write this down in the EMOTIONAL FEELING column. I emphasize *feeling* because anxiety

isn't just a cognitive experience. We feel it in our bodies. Your triggers may evoke feelings of nervousness, anxiety, disgust, hurt, anger, or dread. Give the feeling a name. It will help you in your work to bring down your discomfort. You may have complex or contradictory feelings. Record them all. They don't have to be logical. You may have difficulty coming up with a good word to represent how you feel. Don't get hung up on this; just start with the relatively easy words like mad, bad, sad, and glad. Yes, you can even have discomfort when you are glad.

4. In the next column record the specific THOUGHTS that came to you as a result of the trigger. If you were not aware of any specific thoughts, write a description of what you now think, believe, or imagine when you reflect on the trigger. Don't clean up your internal language when you make the entry. Also, if you use colorful descriptions in your thinking or make absolute statements in your thinking such as never, always, a million times, etc., don't edit—just write what you thought. You need to identify distortions. Right now, it will help to start seeing what you think. Writing it out helps you see in more than just the visual sense.

5. Keep your log for at least several days. If you are in counseling, take your log to the next counseling session and continue to do so. First, this should provide a good baseline assessment of your triggers and stress, and second, it will provide examples of specific situations, thoughts, and events that trigger much of your stress. Continuing to record stress will let you see where more work may be done and where progress in anxiety management is taking place as you move forward.

6. Keep this information to help in identifying triggers, thoughts, and emotions you will use in the exercises below.

PART 3

* * *

YOUR WRITTEN EXPOSURE

Chapter 6

Preparing to Write Your Fears

Obsessive thoughts and compulsive-thought rituals can't be observed by others. Since they aren't physical, coming up with a strategy that exposes a person to the feared stimulus condition makes exposure somewhat challenging. If a counselor suggests imaginal exposure as homework, there would be no hard evidence of homework completion. If we think of the frequency and duration of homework as we do medicine, we would have no evidence of how many doses were taken or how large the doses were. However, if we ask the client to write out his anxiety triggers and his fears of what might happen, we get a very good idea from the length of the handwritten material exactly how large and how frequently the doses of exposure were taken. It turns out that writing the anxiety triggers and narrative stories of feared outcomes carries several other advantages.

When you write your thoughts down on paper or computer you capture them. Now, instead of having obsessive or fear-evoking thoughts float in and out of your mind, you can *see* what you're thinking. Most people with obsessions or excessive worry recognize their thoughts are distorted or even ridiculous, but writing their fears helps them gain more perspective. Note that writing down your fear-evoking thoughts (or doing any exposure exercise) can stir up a lot of anxiety. Some clients believe that writing their fear-evoking thoughts will make the thoughts come true (magical thinking). This shows how powerful and palpable thoughts can become. However, stirring up anxiety by facing fear-evoking triggers and worst-case scenarios is just what we want to do. Habituation to triggers and fear-evoking thoughts cannot be accomplished without exposure. By writing them out, we can control the level of exposure, the duration, and the frequency.

Before you begin your writing exercises, let's look at two writing examples similar to what clients have written.

Client writing examples

We usually tell clients something like "Okay, you have roughly a 75 percent chance of getting a handle on your fears, and you are ready to invest your time. Make sure that you are ready to go all the way with this activity before you begin. We would hate for you to try this for a day or two or five and drop out because it's inconvenient or doesn't seem to be working for you." There seems to be a *tipping point* for many psychotherapeutic interventions. If you stop short of the recommended *dosing*, you may never find out for yourself if it will work for you. What if you stop writing and were only two or three days from noticing a large reduction in your anxiety in response to your triggers? There is no guarantee this approach will help you, but if your brain works like most others, you stand a good chance of reducing your anxiety. This is hard work. If you can't make a commitment to stick with it, put this workbook down and set it aside. Wait until you have the motivation to stick with it. Talk it over with your counselor and discuss smaller steps, alternative types of exposure, and coping techniques. Maybe the two of you can come up with a plan that increases the probability of staying with an exposure exercise.

We often ask clients to write the first narratives of their fears (we often call these worst-case scenarios) with us in the office in order to make sure they understand what to do. While we don't grade the exercise, and we certainly don't care how well somebody writes, we do want clients to get the most out of their effort. Let's take a look at how a person with a fear of hurting somebody's feelings might approach the task of writing his fears away.

First, we ask the individual to list and estimate a SUD rating of the triggers that evoke his anxiety. Here is a college student's list. A word or phrase can be used as a short-form reference for the trigger (words in parentheses).

Examples of writing triggers and worst-case scenarios

Our college student is ready to begin his writing assignment. If he begins with moderate-level SUDs items, he can choose any or all of the items rated from four to six. The simple act of writing the triggers over and over again provides exposure over and over again. Notice we used the trigger's short-form name. The student could write:

> *friend left out, best friend, professor mad, joke hurt feelings, friend left out, best friend, professor mad, joke hurt feelings, friend left out, best friend, professor mad, joke hurt feelings, friend left out, best friend, professor mad, joke hurt feelings, friend left out, best friend, professor mad, joke hurt feelings, etc.*

Triggers	Subjective Units of
Girlfriend's frown (frown)	8
Friend pauses a long time in conversation (pause)	7
Girlfriend doesn't text for two hours or more (no text)	9
Parents upset about my grades (low grades)	9
Friend fails to speak when passing on campus (friends ignore)	7
Making a joke with friends and thinking	6
Answer given in class may have made the professor unhappy	6
Forgot to call and invite a friend to join other friends for lunch	5
Haven't stayed in contact with high school best friend (best	4
I'm not being the best person I can be (offending God)	9

Thinking about these triggers repeatedly as he writes them provides exposure repeatedly. He could write the triggers for ninety minutes, but we want him to imagine where the triggers lead and write out his worst fears. His writing may go something like this:

I saw Jake on the quad, and I thought we should get some friends together before the football game on Saturday. We could get something to eat and go to the stadium and have our usual fun with our nonfraternity friends. Jake was going to call a couple of people, and I was going to call a couple and let them know our plans. Cara has been hanging out with us lately, but I didn't think about calling her to join us until we got to the restaurant and Jake asked me if Cara was coming. I felt embarrassed because I hadn't thought to call her. Jake didn't say anything, but I could tell that he was disappointed. I wanted to apologize, but my counselor said I should resist my urge to apologize, even if I thought it was legitimate, since I seem to compulsively apologize until friends feel irritated with me. For the rest of the night, Jake didn't seem to be having quite as much fun as he usually does. I thought he looked at me in a funny way all night, and I kept thinking I should apologize. I thought he and my other friends talked more to each other and not as much to me. We went to the game. I was afraid we'd see Cara there, and then I'd really feel bad that she wasn't invited. Sure enough, my worst fears were realized when we were sitting there in the stadium, Cara came walking up the steps and was looking right at me. She looked surprised to see us and asked why nobody called her. I knew I was supposed to resist apologizing, so I just told her I forgot to call. She looked hurt, and I could feel my anxiety build as she turned to Jake and said something I couldn't hear. They both just looked at me, and she walked back down the steps. I kept seeing her in the stands below. She didn't seem to be with anybody, and I really felt bad. I wanted to go down to her and apologize, but I continued to resist. Later on in the evening she came back by our group and looked really lonely. I felt so bad that I had let her down. She must think I'm a self-centered and selfish person not to even think to call her to join us.

You may get the idea from this example. The writer should consider as many possible twists and turns the situation can take in order to be as anxious as possible during the exposure. However, our writer didn't quite get his story to the worst-case scenario. Here is one of his worst-case scenarios:

Cara walked over and told Jake and me that she thought we had become pretty good friends and considered herself to be a part of our group. She looked directly at me and said she felt hurt and left out, and wouldn't be having anything to do with me in the future. I thought this would be a place to apologize, but my therapist said I should resist doing that even in what I thought was a legitimate situation. I couldn't think of anything to say that wouldn't be an apology, so I just stood there speechless. She looked at me like she expected me to say something, and when I didn't, she just wiped a tear away and walked away. All of my friends just watched this like they couldn't believe it. They asked me why I hadn't said something to her to apologize. They must think I'm one of the coldest people they know. I think my friends must have said something to other people in our classes because people just don't seem as friendly to me anymore. I feel really bad. I'm really uptight and don't enjoy myself in social situations because I think the word has gotten out that I'm rude and self-centered.

The example above deals with a facet of social anxiety. People with OCD will often have another diagnosable anxiety disorder such as social phobia. With OCD the compulsion for this college student was to apologize. He had apologized so much that his friends got annoyed with him and asked him to stop apologizing and to stop checking to see if they were upset with him. Once exposure started, he was asked not to apologize for any reason for three consecutive days (seventy-two hours). In addition, he was to record the time and circumstances on paper every time he had an urge to apologize. He was asked to note whether he resisted the urge to apologize and when he gave in to the urge.

Let's do another example of exposure writing. The fear of contamination is well known, and we can often create in vivo exposure to common triggers like public toilets, door handles, salad bars, drinking fountains, handrails, and the like. It's not always convenient to do this, however. Transportation to a site to conduct exposure can be an impediment at times. Clients may be reluctant to go into a public facility with a counselor conducting therapy. We definitely want the client to do in vivo exposure, but when it's not convenient, writing worst-case scenarios can provide an effective step in the right direction. Written exposure can also be used to keep this important aspect of treatment going during gaps in schedules with therapists or over weekends or holidays when in vivo exposure cannot be accomplished without assistance. Here is a client's list of contamination triggers:

Triggers	Subjective Units of Discomfort
Toilet seats at home (home toilet)	5
Faucets handles at home (home faucets)	5
Toilet handle at home (toilet handle)	5
Toilet seats in public facilities (public toilet)	10
Faucet handles in public facilities (public faucet)	10
Public door handles (door handles)	8
Table tops in restaurants (table top)	7
Silverware in restaurants (silverware)	6
Shaking hands when introduced (shaking hands)	7
Books and magazines in library (library books)	6
Books and magazines in doctor's office (doctor's magazines)	10
Coughing or sneezing in public (cough/sneeze)	7
Sitting in chair of doctor's office (doctor's chair)	8
Swine flu	10

The person in our current example successfully completed both imaginal and in vivo exposure with the moderately difficult items on the list. She began exposure to the more difficult items using written exposure. Following our example, she repeatedly wrote the following triggers:

doctor's magazines, cough/sneeze, doctor's chair, shaking hands, tabletop, door handles, public faucet, public toilet, doctor's magazines, cough/sneeze, doctor's chair, shaking hands, tabletop, door handles, public faucet, public toilet, etc.

She then began to write a narrative about her worst fears:
I put off going to the doctor's office as long as I can because I hate being in the waiting room with really sick people. The news is always talking about swine flu. I'm right in the age group of the people most likely to get it. I have a regular physical scheduled, and I've put it off so much my doctor's office said they won't schedule with me again unless I have my physical. I walk to the end of the street to catch the bus, and a wino comes around the corner and bumps into me. I want to go home and take a shower, but I'll get charged if I miss my appointment. They may drop me as a patient as much as I've rescheduled. I can just feel my skin crawl with whatever disease he may be carrying. My palms get sweaty, and my heart rate goes up. My anxiety is so high I think about turning around again, but I know I'm supposed to resist this. They call it avoidance, and they say it becomes a compulsion just like washing my hands. I get on the bus and accidently touch the handrail. I fumble around to put the token in the machine and drop it on the floor. God knows what has been on some winos feet or if somebody stepped in dog mess when they walked across the grass. I think I'm going to have a heart attack because I'm feeling so anxious about all these germs. I can't believe I don't even have any hand cleaner. Now I'm stuck on this bus, and these dirty little kids are sitting right across from me. I watch one of them wipe his nose with his hand and then grab the handrail. Did I touch that handrail? I think I'm going to get sick. These kids are about the age of those kids the news said had cases of swine flu. If anybody can catch anything, I'll be sure to get it. I get to the doctor's office, and it's crowded. There is one chair available, and I wonder who was sitting there previously. I started to just stand, but the nurse said to have a seat, and we'll get you to update your personal information. So, I sit in the chair, and I just know somebody may have been exposed to swine flu. I hear somebody sneeze and cough. This is a nightmare. I feel like I'm getting warm. I can't stand these feelings of anxiety. I wonder if I've already been contaminated. I'm feeling flush and a little nauseous. I'm sure I have flu symptoms.

You can see that she's doing a pretty good job of capturing some of her fears, but she still hasn't gotten to the worst-case scenario. Here is one of her examples of a worst-case scenario:

I went to the doctor's office to get vaccinated against swine flu. They say you're not supposed to be able to catch it from the vaccination, but I feel like I have flu symptoms. I take my temperature and I do have a fever of 101. I called my doctor's office, and they're closed today. She's on vacation. I decide to go to an urgent care clinic. I'm feeling weak and tired, and I'm afraid I have swine flu. The urgent care doctor told me he thought I had flulike symptoms. He swabbed my nose and throat and said he'd send the sample to the lab. He told me to go home, and drink plenty of fluids and rest. I went home, and I just felt hotter and sicker. I took my temperature, and sure enough it hit 102. I called the urgent care doctor, and he was off his shift, so I decided to go to the emergency room. They took one look at me and saw how sick I was, so they admitted me to the hospital. Now, I'm really worried about dying. This all started because I thought getting a vaccination would help. It looks like my good intentions are going to kill me. They're pumping fluid into me and giving me medicine. I think I've developed pneumonia. My doctor came back from vacation, and she tells me I'm in pretty bad shape. I should let my family know how bad it is because it could be fatal.

The worst-case scenario could be that she fails to reach her family and dies all alone in a strange hospital bed. However, everybody has a little different take on what their worst-case scenario may be. Following the therapeutic plan, clients continue to work their way up the list of triggers and eventually include the moderately high SUD level (seven) to the highest SUD of ten. Our examples are much shorter than a ninety-minute session, but they should help you begin to get the idea.

Our clients with mild to moderate levels of anxiety and without anxiety disorders tend to find they quickly benefit from the same type of exposure we use with our clients who suffer from anxiety disorders. To get the complete benefit of exposure, clients move on to in vivo exposure looking for opportunities to confront their fears repeatedly until their SUD level reaches two or less. Most find in vivo exposure much easier to face because of the work they've done in writing out their fears.

Exercise: Identify your anxiety triggers

When developing an exposure strategy for OCD, specific phobia, or other anxiety disorder, we catalog every trigger, intrusive thought, or situation that evokes an anxiety response. Now that you have identified some of your anxiety triggers from your stress log and other exercises, you can begin developing a list and prepare for the next step of exposure.

Below, make your list of triggers and beside every item rate the level of anxiety or discomfort you experience with each trigger on a scale of one to ten. Remember, we call these ratings subjective units of discomfort or SUD. A SUD rating of ten represents the highest level of discomfort and a SUD rating of one represents very little discomfort at all. Items within the four to six range would be considered moderately anxiety provoking. The moderate range is the starting point of exposure therapy for most people. There isn't any evidence that starting with a high, moderate, or low level of discomfort works best. Most people are more comfortable beginning with something that doesn't appear overpowering, and yet they want to move as quickly as they can. Therefore, we usually begin with items in the four to six range.

Triggers	Subjective Units of Discomfort (1-10)

Writing Instructions

Instructions can vary from client to client, but the core writing activity includes handwriting (not usually typing) in narrative fashion exactly what you fear will happen when triggers, intrusive thoughts, or obsessions occur. Some clients type and report that they seem to do just as well as when they use longhand. However, we recommend that you sit down and write exclusively about what you fear for at least ninety minutes. Begin by writing about a fear that evokes a SUD of four to six. If you do not have ninety minutes to write, you should write until your fear subsides to at least 50 percent of what you felt when your anxiety hit its peak.

It's just fine to write the same narrative over again. Continue to write your triggers and fears in as many situations as you can imagine until you can no longer get your anxiety above a two or three on the SUD scale. Then, move on to items with SUD levels rated above six. Continue the same procedure until your triggers no longer evoke anxiety above a two or three.

To get the most from exposure, you should continue to write your triggers, your fears and obsessive thoughts including your worst fears. Ultimately, you will write your worst fears and extend them to the worst-case scenario. Even if you know intellectually that the worst-case scenario will never happen you should write it down. You want your brain to have the experience of thinking clearly about the worst-case scenario. Let the anxiety go up; in fact try to take the anxiety up as high as it will go or as much as you can stand. Anxiety will eventually go down. Your brain cannot sustain an intense level of fear forever. The intensity will eventually drop off. You may be worn out when you have completed the exposure task, but you will have taken one step closer to significantly reducing your anxiety long term.

Do the same activity on day two, three, four, and so on for at least fifteen days. If you cannot find the time to devote to the activity, remember that if you're spending at least one hour every day worrying, obsessing, and/or engaging in ritual behaviors or have at least eight intrusive, anxiety-provoking thoughts per day, you might want to give that time over to something that has been found so helpful to others who have suffered with very high levels of anxiety. You may have a three-in-four chance of significantly reducing your anxiety plus the very good chance your fears will occupy much less of your precious time.

Don't stop just because you get bored. Most of us will forget to take medicine when we start to get over an illness because we feel better and just don't remember to do it. Many of us have old antibiotics in our medicine cabinets for that reason. Stay with exposure and do booster sessions until you've kicked your triggers out the door. If you stop short of habituation, you may have to begin exposure all over again for specific triggers or thoughts.

Exercise: Write your fears

Now it's time to begin writing your fears away. Start as we did in the examples above by writing your triggers over and over. Then begin writing in narrative fashion as if you are telling a story about what you fear will happen. Begin writing here and continue your writing in the note section of this workbook or in a separate notebook, so that you can track your progress over time. Continue written exposure until your SUD level lowers to about two. Refer to the example narratives above to make sure you have a clear understanding of what to do. Remember, your writing should contain no coping thoughts or positive outcomes. This writing should focus on what you are afraid might happen. If you can tolerate the discomfort, go ahead and write the worst-case scenario related to the triggers you include in your narrative.

_____
_____
_____
_____
_____
_____
_____
_____
_____
_____
_____
_____
_____
_____

Continue writing your narratives in the notes section included in the appendix of this workbook, or obtain as many composition books you need to continue this exercise until you have decreased your SUD levels on all trigger items to about a SUD level two.

PART 4

✻ ✻ ✻

KEEPING YOUR FEARS AT BAY

Chapter 7

Relapse Prevention

Once you have managed to reduce your anxiety in response to triggers to a SUD level of two, you will want to keep them at bay through repeated exposure. Earlier, I wrote about *in vivo exposure*. The work you've completed in writing your fears away (imaginal exposure) can provide a good basis for constructing a plan for in vivo exposure. You have a list of triggers from which to begin in vivo exposure. There are many references for developing a hierarchy and engaging in exposure and cognitive restructuring for coping with fears.[17]

For many clients without anxiety disorders, use of writing exposure reduces their experience of anxiety to an extent that facing their fears in the real world is much less difficult. For example, being assertive with a relative, making an oral presentation, asking for a date, or going to a social event alone may be much less anxiety provoking. This workbook focuses only on the use of imaginal exposure through writing.

How often and how long should you repeat exposure writing your worst-case scenarios? We don't have any way to truly answer that question for everybody. We do know that disorders such as OCD never go away. Symptoms will wax and wane, but results of cognitive behavior therapy have demonstrated a long-lasting change following treatment. In CBT we always work toward cognitive change and relapse prevention.

Keeping fears at bay includes learning how to change dysfunctional patterns of thinking, distorted and irrational thoughts. A tenet of CBT is that much anxiety and depression is the result of irrational, distorted, and dysfunctional thinking. Therapists work with clients in identifying these dysfunctional thoughts and core beliefs, and then adapting more rational core beliefs and thoughts to deal with real time stress. One of the techniques I use to help my clients identify dysfunctional thoughts is the GOFAR technique.

Identifying and Changing Dysfunctional Thinking with GOFAR

Emotions are created by thoughts or cognitions including what we imagine, believe, or remember. If you log your stress as I have suggested, you can begin to see the very direct connection between thoughts (including your visual imagination, memories, beliefs, and self talk) and your feelings. The thinking part of our brains (neocortex) is connected to the feeling part of our brain (limbic system), so that what we think about, imagine, believe, or remember directly affects what we feel. Therefore, if our thinking is exaggerated, distorted, or dysfunctional, our emotions will also be exaggerated, distorted, or dysfunctional. Through repetition, we develop emotional responses that become automatic. We notice our feeling-reactions to situations much more quickly than we become aware of what we think about those situations.

Our objective, through cognitive behavior therapy, is to bring our feeling-reactions more into line with what is functional and rational for us. The GOFAR acronym represents the criteria we are going to use to help accomplish this. Each criterion represented by letters in the acronym is presented in the form of a question. The possible answer to each question is yes, no, or neutral. No answers represent dysfunctional or irrational thinking. A no answer to any of the five criterion questions automatically suggests that our thinking is not functional or rational and challenges us to generate alternative ways of thinking in response to the stressful event.

Let's do an exercise in analyzing thoughts associated with a stressful event. Refer to the form below to follow along with the way my clients learn how to use the GOFAR analysis. Assume that I have anxious and angry reactions when driving in traffic, and the result has been that people don't really want to ride with me. I need to get a handle on my reactions if I want people to ride with me when I drive. Here is an example of how I may begin to identify my irrational thinking.

Imagine that I was driving seventy miles per hour on the interstate when a van turned in front of me, and the driver slammed on his brakes causing me to brake hard and skid. I felt anxiety and anger. I think, "What an idiot! People like that shouldn't be allowed to drive! I ought to cut him off and see how he likes that."

My goal is to learn how to manage my reactions, so people will feel comfortable traveling with me in the future, and I want to reach my destination safely.

The G in the GOFAR analysis represents the word *GOAL*. My internal test of whether a thought is functional for me is to ask myself the question "Does this thought help me to reach my goal(s)?" Obviously, I need to know what my goal is in this situation. We often do not stop to think about what our goals are when we encounter stressful events. This is one reason we find it hard to change old emotional reactions. My goal was to get to my destination safely and manage my angry reactions, so it is apparent that the thought, "What an idiot…" doesn't help me in any way. It is clearly not goal directed. So, my answer to the first internal test or question is no. I check no in the form below.

The O part of GOFAR represents the word *OTHERS*. The question "Does my thinking help me to get along with others?" is my next internal test. This is a clear no. My thinking would certainly engender anger or hostility toward the other driver. If I react by yelling or attempting to teach the other driver a lesson by cutting him off, any passengers riding with me will feel uncomfortable or scared by my reaction.

The F in GOFAR represents *FEELING*. The question is "Does my thought keep me feeling the way I prefer to feel?" Since I don't like the feeling of anger, my answer to this question is no.

The A in GOFAR stands for the word, *ALIVE*. The question is "Does my thought help keep me alive?" If I am not threatening myself or others, there is probably not a risk to staying alive, so my answer in this case is probably neutral.

The R in GOFAR represents the word *REALITY*. The internal test is to ask myself the question "Is my thought in line with objective reality?" Is the person an idiot? Technically, an idiot would not be able to obtain a driver's license. No, the person is not an idiot. Is the person behaving in a manner similar to what I believe an idiot might? Probably, but the person is not an idiot. More likely, the person is a fallible human being. The fact is I don't know the cause of the person's driving pattern, and it is simply not functional for me to denigrate the person or upset myself about his driving habits any further.

I have answered all of my internal tests. Reviewing the GOFAR analysis form, I can see that I answered four of the questions, no, and one question, neutral. For the sake of learning how to think more functionally and rationally, my task is to think in such a way that I will not receive a no answer to any of the five questions making up the GOFAR acronym. Based on my assessment, there is strong evidence that my thinking is clearly not functional or rational for me. If I received even one no, my challenge is the same. That is, to determine what thoughts I need to develop in order to think about this situation in a more functional way.

Practice in keeping a log such as we have suggested is useful in developing emotional self-awareness. Taking the step of performing the GOFAR analysis helps us to begin creating awareness of internal criteria to guide our reactions. With practice this becomes more automatic. Since we tend to experience stress around the same types of events, we become more skilled in coping with these stresses. Practicing GOFAR in real time has the effect of enhancing not only our emotional self-awareness but inoculates against stressful reactions in the future.

It takes disciplined practice to develop automatic thinking so that reactions are more functional for us. Many of the people I have worked with in private counseling have increased their skill in emotional regulation by using this strategy. This has resulted in decreasing stress and even recovery from depression and anxiety.

GOFAR Analysis Example

First, enter your SUD level and describe the trigger. SUD (subjective units of discomfort) ranges from 1 to 10 with 10—being as

SUD 7

TRIGGER
Driving 70 on the interstate when a van cut in front of me and slammed on his brakes

Next, enter your thoughts and emotional feelings.

THOUGHTS:
What an idiot! People like that shouldn't be allowed to drive! I ought to cut them off and see how they like that.

EMOTIONAL FEELINGS:

GOFAR ANALYSIS

G. Does my thinking help me to reach my goal(s)?
Yes___ No_X__ Neutral___

O. Does my thinking help me to get along with others?
Yes___ No_X__ Neutral___

F. Does my thinking keep me feeling the way I prefer to feel?
Yes___ No_X__ Neutral___

A. Does my thinking help keep me alive?
Yes___ No___ Neutral_X__

R. Is my thinking in line with objective reality?
Yes___ No_X__ Neutral___

If any of the questions above received a "No," try to generate thoughts that would receive a "Yes" or "Neutral Answer" to each of the criteria. Enter your alternative thinking below.

Functional or Rational Alternative Thought(s)
The person driving the van is creating a dangerous situation. They probably aren't out to get me and just had a lapse in attention. I am better off taking a deep breath and focusing on my own driving.

Exercise: GOFAR analysis

After reviewing the example, try analyzing a stressful situation of your own.

What is your goal in this situation?
_____

Enter you SUD level and describe the trigger.

SUD

TRIGGER:

Enter your thoughts and emotions.

THOUGHTS:

EMOTIONS:

1. Does my thinking help me to reach my goal(s)?
   Yes____ No____ Neutral____

2. Does my thinking help me to get along with others?
   Yes____ No____ Neutral____

3. Does my thinking keep me feeling the way I prefer to feel?
   Yes____ No____ Neutral____

4. Does my thinking help keep me alive?
   Yes____ No____ Neutral____

5. Is my thinking in line with objective reality?
   Yes____ No____ Neutral____

If any of the questions above received a "No," try to generate a thought(s) that would receive a "Yes" or "Neutral Answer" to each of the criteria. Enter your alternative thinking below.

Functional or Rational Alternative Thought(s)

Relapse prevention plan

Relapse prevention is a process that includes taking positive steps to maintain one's health. It is a practical plan that addresses avoiding possible pitfalls that may occur during and following recovery. It is a process that begins well in advance of any act (i.e., binge eating, drinking alcohol, or engaging in obsessive-compulsive behavior). Because relapse factors are unique to each individual, their diagnosis, and their recovery plan, the faster a client can recognize the signals that signal relapse, the faster he or she can take positive action toward recovery. We like to begin developing a relapse prevention plan early in the treatment phase and well before we discontinue active CBT.

The basic elements of a plan include: 1) making a list of healthy behaviors (cognitive and behavioral) or improvement; 2) creating a plan for maintaining these healthy behaviors; 3) identifying and listing signs of relapse; 4) creating a plan of intervention if there are signs of relapse; 5) identifying the most serious signs of relapse; and, 6) creating a plan of steps to take if a full relapse becomes evident.

Anticipating possible relapse doesn't represent a pessimistic view of recovery. It takes substantial insight development and practice to gain mastery over some symptoms such as those in OCD, PTSD, and social phobia. We also know through observation and research that people tend to put aside preventative and protective behaviors when they feel well. For example, patients recovering from a sinus infection will stop remembering to take their antibiotic medication. People in recovery from addictions will think they can use some substances and not completely relapse. People with anxiety disorders will put off exposure because it's not convenient and their symptoms have become less intense. We have come to believe that lapse and relapse should be anticipated, so that a planned response can be initiated and the debilitating effects of symptoms can be minimized as quickly as possible. We don't see lapses and relapses as failure but a common feature in learning how to cope with the complexity of life circumstances.

Healthy behaviors, maintenance, and warning signs will look different for each individual and his particular problems, but some basic signs and steps for preventing relapse based on one client's plan are listed below:

1) **Healthy behaviors or improvement:**
   a) I find my triggers elicit less anxiety and are less frequent (SUD of two or three, eight to ten times per week.
   b) I am able to inhibit my ritual behaviors 99 percent of the time.
   c) I am sleeping better and waking up on time (seven and one-half hours per night).

d) I am feeling more motivated at work and at home (completing tasks at work and keeping house maintained).
   e) I am going out and doing more on a daily basis (grocery shopping, lunch with friends, exercising, etc.).
   f) I have started thinking more positively about things (setting goals, making plans, appreciating my spouse and children etc.).

2) **I will do the following to maintain my healthy behaviors:**
   a) Attend my counseling sessions regularly and do my homework assignments.
   b) Continue to use techniques learned in therapy to help dispute my anxiety provoking thoughts, e.g., "It's just my OCD."
   c) Challenge myself to keep up my exposure.
   d) To engage in rewarding behaviors that I had lost interest in at least once a day (art, reading, music, etc.).
   e) Surround myself with people who can support me.

3) **Warning signs of relapse (condition yellow) include:**
   a) An increase in negative thinking patterns throughout the day (i.e., I'm worthless, nothing will ever workout for me, etc.).
   b) An increase in the frequency of suicidal thinking (i.e., upon the occurrence of suicidal thinking, I will call my mental health professional).
   c) A decrease in daily activity.
   d) Difficulty getting out of bed (i.e., two out of seven times a week).
   e) Not taking medication as recommended by doctor or mental health professional.
   f) Not bathing or keeping hygiene up as well as before.
   g) Skipping therapy sessions and counseling homework occasionally.
   h) Isolating myself from my support group.

4) **I will do the following when I notice condition yellow:**
   a) Begin engaging in behaviors mentioned in 2).
   b) Begin speaking to members of my support group about my struggle.
   c) Call or speak with my mental health professional.

5) **Warning signs of relapse (condition red) include:**
   a) Spontaneously stopping medications or failing to comply with your medical or mental health professionals' recommendations.
   b) Suicidal thoughts and a plan to commit suicide (I will call a mental health professional, go to the emergency room, or call 911 for help.).
   c) Frequent irritability.

d) Hanging around old friends and engaging in situations that trigger certain thoughts or negative behavior.
   e) Insomnia (not feeling rested after waking).
   f) Failure to attend treatment.
   g) Increased sadness.

6) **I will do the following when I notice condition red:**
   a) See my counselor immediately or call the emergency line if I need help after office hours.
   b) Contact someone in my support system who can help me.

Exercise: Develop your relapse prevention plan

I recommend that you develop your own relapse prevention plan using the model above as a reference. I'm a believer in consulting with an expert when necessary. A little support and expert advice may help you see something you've overlooked or provide suggestions that make exposure tasks more approachable.

1) **Healthy behaviors or improvement:**
   Enter a list of signs of health or improvement you see as a result of your work in changing your thinking and behavior:
   a) _____
   b) _____
   c) _____
   d) _____
   e) _____
   f) _____

2) **I will do the following to maintain my healthy behaviors:**
   List the behaviors, people, and strategies you will use to maintain the signs of health in 1).
   a) _____
   b) _____
   c) _____
   d) _____
   e) _____
   f) _____

3) **Warning signs of relapse (condition yellow) include:**
   Identify the behaviors, moods, or situations that would indicate you are beginning to slip back from your current healthy state as in 1).

a) _____
b) _____
c) _____
d) _____
e) _____
f) _____

4) **I will do the following when I notice condition yellow:**
   What steps will you take if you notice you have begun to revert to some old patterns of behavior?
   a) _____
   b) _____
   c) _____
   d) _____
   e) _____
   f) _____

5) **Warning signs of relapse (condition red) include:**
   Identify the behaviors, moods, or situations that would indicate you are beginning to relapse into the pattern of behaviors that led to your work on self-improvement:
   a) _____
   b) _____
   c) _____
   d) _____
   e) _____
   f) _____

6) **I will do the following when I notice condition red:**
   What steps will you take toward recovering your healthy behavior patterns?
   a) _____
   b) _____
   c) _____
   d) _____
   e) _____
   f) _____

Closing

I hope you find this workbook helpful as you work through your stresses, anxiety triggers, and worst-case scenarios in the future. I will appreciate feedback on the content and structure of this workbook. Anything you think will make it more user friendly or helpful to others, please feel free to e-mail me at support@david.barnhart.com.

David L. Barnhart, EdD

Appendix

Writing your fears note pages

Write your fears away

Writing your fears note pages

Write your fears away

Writing your fears note pages

Write your fears away

Writing your fears note pages

Write your fears away

Writing your fears note pages

Write your fears away

References

[1] http://ocfoundation.org/

[2] http://www.hope4ocd.com/gorbis.php

[3] S. Saxena, E. Gorbis, J. O'Neill, S.K. Baker, M.A. Mandelkern, K.M. Maidment, S. Chang, N. Salamon, A.L. Brody, L. M. Schwartz, E.D. London, "Rapid effects of brief intensive cognitive-behavioral therapy on brain glucose metabolism in obsessive-compulsive disorder," *Molecular Psychiatry* 14, 2 (2009): 197-205.

[4] V. Paquette, J. Levesque, B.Mensour, J-M. Leroux, G. Beaudoin, P. Bourgouin, M. Beauregard, Change the mind and you change the brain: Effects of cognitive-behavioral therapy on the neural correlates of spider phobia," *NeuroImage* 18, 2 (2003): 401-409.

[5] J.M. Schwartz, "Neuroanatomical aspects of cognitive-behavioural therapy response in obsessive-compulsive disorder. An evolving perspective on brain and behaviour," *British Journal of Psychiatry* 35 (1998): S38-44.

[6] R.A. Bryant, M.L. Moulds, R.M. Guthrie, R.D.V. Nixon, "The additive benefit of hypnosis and cognitive-behavioral–therapy in treating acute stress disorder, *Journal of Consulting and Clinical Psychology* 73, 2 (2005): 334-240.

[7] N. Paunovic and L.G. Ost, Cognitive-behavior therapy vs. exposure therapy in the treatment of PTSD in refugees. *Behaviour Research and Therapy* 39,10 (2001): 1183-1197.

[8] C.J. Aaronson, M.K. Shear, R.R. Goetz, L.B. Allen, D.H. Barlow, K.S. White, S. Ray, R. Money, J.R. Saksa, S.R. Woods, and J.M. Gorman, "Predictors and time course of response among panic disorder patients treated with cognitive-behavioral therapy," Journal of Clinical Psychology 69, 3 (2008): 418-424.

[9] D.M. Clark, P.M. Salkovskis, A. Hackmann, H. Middleton, P. Ananstasiades, and M. Gelder, "A comparison of cognitive therapy, applied relaxation, and imipramine in the treatment of panic disorder," *British Journal of Psychiatry* 164 (1994): 759-769.

[10] P. Carlbring, L.B. Nordgren, T. Furmark, and G. Andeersson, "Long-term outcome of Internet-delivered cognitive-behavioural therapy for social phobia: a thirty-month follow up," *Behaviour Research and Therapy* 47, 10 (2009): 848-850.

[11] C. Suveg, J.L. Hudson, G. Brewer, E. Schroeder-Flannery, E. Gosch, and P.C. Kendall, Cognitive-behavioral therapy for anxiety-disordered youth: secondary outcomes from a randomized clinical trial evaluating child and family modalities, *Journal of Anxiety Disorders* 23, 3 (2009): 341-349.

[12] Lisa A. Miller, Katherine H. Taber, Glen O. Gabbard, and Robin A. Hurley, "Neural Underpinnings of Fear and Its Modulation: Implications for Anxiety Disorders," *Journal of Neuropsychiatry Clinical Neuroscience* 17 (2005): 1-6.

[13] J.R. Simpson Jr., W.C. Drevets, A.Z. Snyder, D.A. Gusnard, M.E. Raichle, "Emotion-induced changes in medial prefrontal cortex:II During anticipatory anxiety," *PNAS* 98, 2 (2001): 688-693.

[14] P.R. Goldin, T. Manber, S. Hakimi, T. Canli, and J. Gross, "Neural bases social anxiety disorder, emotional reactivity and cognitive regulation during social or physical threat," *Archives of General Psychology* 66, 2 (2009): 170-180.

[15] L. Shin, S. P. Orr, M.A. Carson, S.L. Rauch, "Regional cerebral blood flow in the amygdala and medical prefrontal cortex during traumatic imagery in male and female Vietnam veterans with PTSD," *Archives of General Psychology* 61, 2 (2004): 168-176.

[16] *Merriam-Webster Online Dictionary,* accessed 26 September 2009, http://www.merriam-webster.com/dictionary/worry.

[17] http://ocfoundation.org/

Made in the USA
Columbia, SC
27 June 2018